foreword

It's a classic chicken-and-egg question: did all the great chicken fingers, nuggets, sandwiches and easy entrees cause our white-meat love affair, or was it the other way around?

Whatever the answer, it's safe to say that boneless, skinless chicken breasts are what busy adults grab when they want to put something nutritious and appealing on the table fast. Kids adore the taste, and guests from around the world enjoy its versatility. Broiled, braised or baked, placed under exotic sauces or over garlicky salads, chicken's white meat is a hit with everyone.

We've assembled some of our most tempting chicken breast recipes in this helpful little book, with family-friendly dishes at the beginning, and more elaborate, entertainment fare toward the back. Try them all, and see how easy it is to finesse dinnertime success with these delicious chicken breast meals.

Jean Paré

chicken wraps

Since you've already got the barbecue going, you can lightly brush the tortillas with cooking oil and heat them on the grill just before you assemble these wraps.

Chopped fresh cilantro or parsley (or 1 tbsp., 15 mL, dried)	1/4 cup	60 mL
Cooking oil	3 tbsp.	50 mL
Garlic cloves, minced (or 1/2 tsp., 2 mL, powder)	2	2
Ground cumin	1 tsp.	5 mL
Dried crushed chilies (optional)	2 tsp.	10 mL
Boneless, skinless chicken breast halves	1 lb.	454 g
Lime juice	1/4 cup	60 mL
Corn relish	1/4 cup	60 mL
Sour cream	1/4 cup	60 mL
Flour tortillas (9 inch, 22 cm, diameter)	4	4
Ripe large avocado, sliced	1	1
Medium red pepper, thinly sliced	1	1
Grated medium Cheddar cheese	1 cup	250 mL

Combine first 5 ingredients in medium bowl.

Add chicken. Turn to coat. Chill, covered, for at least 1 hour, turning occasionally.

Add lime juice. Stir. Drain and discard liquid. Preheat gas barbecue to medium. Cook chicken on greased grill for 10 to 15 minutes per side until no longer pink inside. Cut across the grain into 1/4 inch (6 mm) slices. Cover to keep warm.

Combine corn relish and sour cream in small bowl. Spread evenly on tortillas. Layer chicken and remaining 3 ingredients, in order given, along centre of each tortilla, leaving 2 inches (5 cm) at each side. Fold sides over filling. Roll up from bottom to enclose filling. Cut in half diagonally. Serves 8.

1 serving: 299 Calories; 18.0 g Total Fat (7.4 g Mono, 2.4 g Poly, 5.5 g Sat); 51 mg Cholesterol; 16 g Carbohydrate; 2 g Fibre; 19 g Protein; 282 mg Sodium

blackened chicken caesar salad

Blackened cooking originated in New Orleans. Traditionally, meat or fish is rubbed with Cajun spices and then cooked quickly in a hot, greased pan, giving the meat a crisp, dark crust. To speed things up, we've added the spices during cooking, with equally tasty results.

CREAMY CAESAR DRESSING

Grated Parmesan cheese	1/2 cup	125 mL
Cooking oil	3 tbsp.	50 mL
Sour cream	3 tbsp.	50 mL
White wine vinegar	1 tbsp.	15 mL
Lemon juice	1 tsp.	5 mL
Worcestershire sauce	1 tsp.	5 mL
Garlic salt	1/2 tsp.	2 mL
Pepper	1/4 tsp.	1 mL

BLACKENED CHICKEN

Cooking oil	1 tbsp.	15 mL
Boneless, skinless chicken breast halves, cut into 3/4 inch (2 cm) pieces	2 lbs.	900 g
Ketchup	2 tbsp.	30 mL
Paprika	1 tbsp.	15 mL
Cayenne pepper	1/2 tsp.	2 mL
Chili powder	1/2 tsp.	2 mL
Ground thyme	1/2 tsp.	2 mL
Onion powder	1/2 tsp.	2 mL
Salt	2 tsp.	10 mL
Pepper	1/2 tsp.	2 mL
Heads of romaine lettuce, cut or torn	2	2
Croutons	1 cup	250 mL
Grated Parmesan cheese	1/4 cup	60 mL
Grated Parmesan cheese, for garnish		

Creamy Caesar Dressing: Combine all 8 ingredients in small bowl. Chill, covered, for 10 minutes to blend flavours. Makes about 1/2 cup (125 mL) dressing.

Blackened Chicken: Heat wok or large frying pan on medium-high until very hot. Add cooking oil. Add chicken. Stir-fry for 6 to 7 minutes until chicken is lightly browned.

Add next 8 ingredients. Stir-fry for 8 to 10 minutes until chicken is no longer pink. Remove from heat.

Put next 3 ingredients into large bowl. Toss. Drizzle with dressing. Toss. Arrange on 8 dinner plates. Scatter chicken mixture over top.

Garnish with second amount of cheese. Serves 8.

1 serving: 290 Calories; 13.9 g Total Fat (6.2 g Mono, 2.9 g Poly, 3.7 g Sat); 75 mg Cholesterol; 9 g Carbohydrate; 2 g Fibre; 32 g Protein; 983 mg Sodium

chicken and artichoke salad

Family and friends will want seconds of this main-course salad, but if any leftovers remain, pack them for lunch the next day.

BALSAMIC MARINADE

Olive (or cooking) oil	1/3 cup	75 mL
Balsamic vinegar	1/4 cup	60 mL
Liquid honey	2 tbsp.	30 mL
Chopped fresh basil (or 3/4 tsp., 4 mL, dried)	1 tbsp.	15 mL
Garlic cloves, minced (or 1/2 tsp., 2 mL, powder)	2	2
Lemon pepper	1 tsp.	5 mL
Boneless, skinless chicken breast halves	3/4 lb.	340 g

SALAD

Large red onion, cut into 8 wedges	1	1
Fresh spinach leaves, lightly packed	3 1/2 cups	875 mL
Can of artichoke hearts, drained and coarsely chopped	14 oz.	398 mL
Cherry tomatoes, halved	1 cup	250 mL
Chopped walnuts, toasted (see Tip, page 64)	1 cup	250 mL
Crumbled feta cheese	3/4 cup	175 mL

Balsamic Marinade: Combine all 6 ingredients in jar with tight-fitting lid. Shake well. Makes about 3/4 cup (175 mL) marinade.

Put chicken into large resealable freezer bag. Add half of marinade. Seal bag. Turn to coat. Let stand in refrigerator for 3 hours. Remove chicken. Preheat gas barbecue to medium. Cook chicken on greased grill for about 10 to 15 minutes per side until no longer pink inside. Chop coarsely. Transfer to large bowl.

Salad: Cook onion on greased grill for about 10 minutes, turning once, until softened and grill marks appear. Add to chicken. Add remaining 5 ingredients. Toss. Drizzle reserved marinade over top. Toss. Makes about 11 cups (2.75 L). Serves 6.

1 serving: 369 Calories; 24.4 g Total Fat (8.7 g Mono, 9.3 g Poly, 4.9 g Sat); 58 mg Cholesterol; 15 g Carbohydrate; 4 g Fibre; 26 g Protein; 459 mg Sodium

chicken hotpot

Sometimes known as Chinese cabbage, bok choy looks more like a cross between celery and Romaine lettuce. While it's frequently found in stir fries and soups, you can also eat the white stalks raw with your favourite dip.

Cooking oil	2 tsp.	10 mL
Boneless, skinless chicken breast halves, chopped	3/4 lb.	340 g
Sliced carrot	1 cup	250 mL
Sliced fresh shiitake mushrooms	1 cup	250 mL
Can of shoestring-style bamboo shoots, drained	8 oz.	227 mL
Prepared chicken broth	1/4 cup	60 mL
Rice vinegar	1/4 cup	60 mL
Soy sauce	2 tbsp.	30 mL
Granulated sugar	2 tsp.	10 mL
Finely grated gingerroot	1 tsp.	5 mL
Sesame oil (for flavour)	1 tsp.	5 mL
Pepper	1/2 tsp.	2 mL
Chopped bok choy	2 cups	500 mL
Chopped red pepper	1 cup	250 mL
Water	2 tbsp.	30 mL
Cornstarch	1 tbsp.	15 mL

Heat cooking oil in large saucepan on medium-high. Add chicken. Cook, uncovered, for 2 to 4 minutes, stirring occasionally, until no longer pink.

Add next 10 ingredients. Stir. Bring to a boil. Reduce heat to medium. Boil gently, partially covered, for 2 to 4 minutes until carrot is almost tender-crisp.

Add bok choy and red pepper. Stir. Cook, covered, for 2 to 4 minutes until vegetables are tender-crisp.

Stir water into cornstarch in small cup. Add to chicken mixture. Heat and stir until boiling and thickened. Makes about 6 cups (1.5 L). Serves 4.

1 serving: 189 Calories; 5.3 g Total Fat (2.1 g Mono, 1.7 g Poly, 0.8 g Sat); 49 mg Cholesterol; 13 g Carbohydrate; 3 g Fibre; 23 g Protein; 543 mg Sodium

lemon chicken and sauce

The sauce takes on a pretty pink colour from the grenadine. Don't forget to eat the lettuce—it's delightfully refreshing with lemon sauce on it! Rice and grilled vegetables can finish the meal.

LEMON MARINADE

Frozen concentrated lemonade, thawed	1/4 cup	60 mL
Cooking oil	1 tbsp.	15 mL
Grenadine syrup	1 tbsp.	15 mL
Onion powder	1/2 tsp.	2 mL
Garlic salt	1/2 tsp.	2 mL
Boneless, skinless chicken breast halves	4	4

LEMON SAUCE

Water	1/2 cup	125 mL
Frozen concentrated lemonade, thawed	1/4 cup	60 mL
Grenadine syrup	2 tbsp.	30 mL
Cornstarch	1 tbsp.	15 mL
Grated lemon zest	1 tsp.	5 mL
Chopped or torn iceberg lettuce, lightly packed	2 cups	500 mL
Lemon slices, halved, for garnish		

Lemon Marinade: Combine first 5 ingredients in small bowl. Makes about 1/3 cup (75 mL) marinade.

Put chicken into large resealable freezer bag. Add marinade. Seal bag. Turn until coated. Let stand in refrigerator for at least 6 hours or overnight, turning occasionally. Remove chicken. Preheat gas barbecue to medium. Place chicken on greased grill. Close lid. Cook for 20 to 25 minutes, turning occasionally, until no longer pink inside.

Lemon Sauce: Combine next 5 ingredients in small saucepan. Heat and stir on medium for about 6 minutes until boiling and thickened.

Arrange lettuce on 4 plates. Place chicken on lettuce. Spoon sauce over top.

Garnish with lemon slices. Serves 4.

1 serving: 276 Calories; 4.2 g Total Fat (1.6 g Mono, 1.1 g Poly, 0.8 g Sat); 81 mg Cholesterol; 27 g Carbohydrate; trace Fibre; 32 g Protein; 90 mg Sodium

chicken cacciatore

Originally from Italy, this "hunter's style" chicken stew is delicious over noodles or rice.

Cooking oil	1 tbsp.	15 mL
Boneless, skinless chicken breast halves	6	6
Medium onion, chopped	1	1
Garlic cloves, minced (or 1/2 tsp., 2 mL, powder)	2	2
Sliced fresh white mushrooms	2 cups	500 mL
Can of crushed tomatoes	14 oz.	398 mL
Ketchup	2 tbsp.	30 mL
Dried basil	1/2 tsp.	2 mL
Dried oregano	1/2 tsp.	2 mL
Granulated sugar	1/2 tsp.	2 mL
Salt	1/2 tsp.	2 mL
Pepper	1/4 tsp.	1 mL
Water	1 tbsp.	15 mL
Cornstarch	1 tbsp.	15 mL

Heat cooking oil in large frying pan on medium-high. Add chicken. Cook, uncovered, for 2 to 3 minutes per side until browned. Remove to plate. Cover to keep warm.

Add onion and garlic to same frying pan. Cook for about 5 minutes, stirring occasionally, until onion is softened.

Add next 8 ingredients. Stir. Add chicken. Bring to a boil. Reduce heat to medium-low. Simmer, covered, for 20 to 30 minutes, stirring occasionally, until chicken is no longer pink inside. Transfer chicken with slotted spoon to serving plate.

Stir water into cornstarch in small cup. Add to tomato mixture. Heat and stir until boiling and thickened. Spoon over chicken. Serve immediately. Serves 6.

1 serving: 187 Calories; 4.6 g Total Fat (1.9 g Mono, 1.3 g Poly, 0.7 g Sat); 66 mg Cholesterol; 9 g Carbohydrate; 1 g Fibre; 27 g Protein; 369 mg Sodium

chicken breast royale

Assemble this entree in the morning and refrigerate until ready to bake. You can also use frozen chicken breasts; just increase the baking time to two hours. Leave out the gravy browner if you prefer a lighter-coloured sauce.

Boneless, skinless chicken breast halves	8	8
Can of condensed cream of mushroom soup	10 oz.	284 mL
Fat-free sour cream	1 cup	250 mL
Green onions, chopped	6	6
All-purpose flour	1/4 cup	60 mL
Dry (or alcohol-free) white wine	1/4 cup	60 mL
Liquid gravy browner	1/2 tsp.	2 mL
Seasoned salt	1/2 tsp.	2 mL
Paprika	1/4 tsp.	1 mL

Arrange chicken in single layer in greased 9 x 13 inch (22 x 33 cm) pan or small roasting pan.

Combine remaining 8 ingredients in small bowl. Spoon over chicken. Bake, uncovered, in 350°F (175°C) oven for about 1 1/4 hours until chicken is no longer pink inside. Serves 8.

1 serving: 199 Calories; 4.4 g Total Fat (1 g Mono, 1.7 g Poly, 1.2 g Sat); 69 mg Cholesterol; 8 g Carbohydrate; trace Fibre; 29 g Protein; 492 mg Sodium

chicken julienne

When everyone has different schedules, this dish reheats quickly, and kids love it served over split buns or noodles. Cutting something julienne means slicing it into matchstick-sized pieces.

Hard margarine (not butter)	2 tsp.	10 mL
Boneless, skinless chicken breast halves, julienned	1 1/2 lbs.	680 g
Sliced fresh white mushrooms	2 cups	500 mL
Chopped green onion	1/4 cup	60 mL
Evaporated milk (or half-and-half cream)	3/4 cup	175 mL
Dry (or alcohol-free) white wine	1/2 cup	125 mL
Parsley flakes	1 tsp.	5 mL
Salt	1/8 tsp.	0.5 mL
Pepper, sprinkle		

Melt margarine in large frying pan on medium-high. Add next 3 ingredients. Cook, stirring often, for about 3 minutes until chicken is no longer pink. Transfer to medium bowl.

Add evaporated milk and wine to same frying pan. Bring to a boil. Reduce heat to medium. Boil gently, uncovered, until reduced by half. Add next 3 ingredients and chicken mixture. Heat and stir until hot, but not boiling. Makes about 3 1/2 cups (875 mL).

3/4 cup (175 mL): 238 Calories; 3.7 g Total Fat (1.6 g Mono, 0.6 g Poly, 0.9 g Sat); 86 mg Cholesterol; 7 g Carbohydrate; 0.6 g Fibre; 38 g Protein; 245 mg Sodium

thai coconut chicken

By using lower-fat ingredients, you can enjoy this delicious Thai dish without any guilt!

Prepared chicken broth	1 1/4 cups	300 mL
Lime juice (see Tip, page 64)	3 tbsp.	50 mL
Soy sauce	2 tbsp.	30 mL
Finely grated gingerroot	1 tbsp.	15 mL
Grated lime zest	1 tbsp.	15 mL
Garlic cloves, minced (or 1/2 tsp., 2 mL, powder)	2	2
Pepper	1/4 tsp.	1 mL
Boneless, skinless chicken breast halves	4	4
Brown sugar, packed	1/4 cup	60 mL
Reduced-fat peanut butter	2 tbsp.	30 mL
Sweet chili sauce	1 tbsp.	15 mL
Light coconut milk	1/2 cup	125 mL
Cornstarch	2 tsp.	10 mL

Grated lime zest, for garnish

Combine first 7 ingredients in medium frying pan. Bring to a boil. Reduce heat to medium.

Add chicken. Cook, covered, for 12 to 15 minutes, turning at halftime, until chicken is no longer pink inside. Transfer chicken to serving plate. Cover to keep warm.

Whisk next 3 ingredients into broth mixture until smooth. Bring to a boil.

Stir coconut milk into cornstarch in small cup. Slowly add to broth mixture, stirring constantly with whisk, until boiling and slightly thickened. Serve with chicken.

Garnish with lime zest. Serves 4.

1 serving: 304 Calories; 7.6 g Total Fat (0.7 g Mono, 0.7 g Poly, 2.7 g Sat); 82 mg Cholesterol; 22 g Carbohydrate; 1 g Fibre; 35 g Protein; 1012 mg Sodium

easy chicken paprikash

In Hungary, red peppers—both hot and sweet—grow abundantly and are dried to create the country's famous paprika powder. Use the freshest possible for a true central European experience. Delicious served over buttered egg noodles.

All-purpose flour	1/4 cup	60 mL
Paprika	1 tbsp.	15 mL
Salt	1 tsp.	5 mL
Boneless, skinless chicken breast halves, cut into 1 inch (2.5 cm) cubes	1 lb.	454 g
Cooking oil	1 tbsp.	15 mL
Cooking oil	2 tsp.	10 mL
Chopped green pepper	1 cup	250 mL
Chopped onion	1 cup	250 mL
Can of diced tomatoes (with juice)	14 oz.	398 mL
Prepared chicken broth	1/2 cup	125 mL
Apple juice	2 tbsp.	30 mL
Dried dillweed	2 tsp.	10 mL
Sour cream	1/3 cup	75 mL
Sprigs of fresh dill, for garnish		

Combine first 3 ingredients in medium resealable freezer bag. Add chicken. Seal bag. Toss until coated.

Heat first amount of cooking oil in large frying pan on medium-high. Add chicken. Set aside any remaining flour mixture. Cook for about 5 minutes, turning at halftime, until browned. Transfer to plate. Cover to keep warm.

Add second amount of cooking oil to same frying pan. Reduce heat to medium. Add green pepper and onion. Cook for 2 to 4 minutes, stirring occasionally, until vegetables are tender-crisp. Add chicken and reserved flour mixture. Stir.

Add next 4 ingredients. Stir. Bring to a boil. Reduce heat to medium-low. Simmer, covered, for about 5 minutes, stirring occasionally, until vegetables are softened and chicken is no longer pink inside.

Add sour cream. Stir.

Garnish with dill sprigs. Makes about 5 cups (1.25 L). Serves 4.

Per Serving: 239 Calories; 10.3 g Total Fat (4.5 g Mono, 2.2 g Poly, 2.9 g Sat); 59 mg Cholesterol; 15 g Carbohydrate; 1 g Fibre; 22 g Protein; 820 mg Sodium

chicken breast supreme

Crispy and golden on the outside; moist and flavourful inside, this chicken is supremely tasty. It's also surprisingly low-fat because it's baked, rather than deep-fried.

Fat-free sour cream	1 cup	250 mL
Lemon juice	2 tbsp.	30 mL
Garlic clove, minced (or 1/4 tsp., 1 mL, powder)	1	1
Celery salt	1 tsp.	5 mL
Paprika	1 tsp.	5 mL
Worcestershire sauce	1 tsp.	5 mL
Salt	1 tsp.	5 mL
Pepper	1/4 tsp.	1 mL
Boneless, skinless chicken breast halves	6	6
Cornflakes cereal, coarsely crushed (not crumbs)	1 3/4 cups	425 mL
Hard margarine (or butter), melted	3 tbsp.	50 mL

Combine first 8 ingredients in small bowl. Put chicken into large resealable freezer bag. Pour sour cream mixture over chicken. Seal bag. Turn until coated. Let stand in refrigerator for at least 6 hours or overnight. Remove chicken.

Put cornflake crumbs into small shallow dish. Press both sides of chicken into cornflake crumbs until coated. Arrange on greased baking sheet. Let stand, covered, in refrigerator for 1 to 2 hours for a crispier coating.

Drizzle with melted margarine. Bake in 350°F (175°C) oven for about 1 hour until no longer pink inside. Serves 6.

1 serving: 255 Calories; 6.9 g Total Fat (3.9 g Mono, 0.9 g Poly, 1.5 g Sat); 68 mg Cholesterol; 10 g Carbohydrate; trace Fibre; 29 g Protein; 931 mg Sodium

orange cumin chicken

Don't be foiled by late meetings and rush hour traffic! These foil packets of flavourful chicken will be on the table in half an hour! (You can even assemble these in the morning before you leave for work.)

Frozen concentrated orange juice, thawed	1/4 cup	60 mL
Brown sugar, packed	1 tbsp.	15 mL
Ground cumin	1 tsp.	5 mL
Garlic powder	1/2 tsp.	2 mL
Ground cinnamon	1/2 tsp.	2 mL
Ground ginger	1/2 tsp.	2 mL
Sesame oil (for flavour)	1/2 tsp.	2 mL
Salt	1/2 tsp.	2 mL
Pepper	1/2 tsp.	2 mL
Boneless, skinless chicken breast halves	4	4

Sprigs of fresh parsley, for garnish

Combine first 9 ingredients in small bowl.

Cut 4 sheets of heavy-duty (or double layer of regular) foil, each about 14 inches (35 cm) long. Place 1 piece of chicken in centre of each sheet. Spoon orange juice mixture over top. Fold edges of foil together over chicken to enclose. Fold ends to seal completely. Place packets, seam-side up, on ungreased baking sheet. Bake in 450°F (220°C) oven for 18 to 20 minutes until chicken is no longer pink inside.

Garnish with parsley sprigs. Serves 4.

1 serving: 179 Calories; 2.6 g Total Fat (0.7 g Mono, 0.7 g Poly, 0.6 g Sat); 66 mg Cholesterol; 11 g Carbohydrate; trace Fibre; 26 g Protein; 358 mg Sodium

whimsical chicken

This dish is such a family pleaser that your kids won't mind helping. Let them do the dipping and breading while you prepare a salad.

Hard margarine (or butter), melted	1/3 cup	75 mL
Salad dressing (or mayonnaise)	1/3 cup	75 mL
Prepared mustard	1 1/2 tbsp.	25 mL
Paprika	1 tsp.	5 mL
Parsley flakes	1 tsp.	5 mL
Salt	3/4 tsp.	4 mL
Pepper	1/4 tsp.	1 mL
Fine dry bread crumbs	1 cup	250 mL
Boneless, skinless chicken breast halves, pounded flat	8	8

Combine first 7 ingredients in small bowl.

Put bread crumbs into small shallow dish.

Dip chicken in salad dressing mixture. Press both sides into bread crumbs until coated. Arrange in single layer on ungreased baking sheet. Bake in 325°F (160°C) oven for about 1 1/2 hours until no longer pink inside. Serves 8.

1 serving: 307 Calories; 14.8 g Total Fat (8.3 g Mono, 3.0 g Poly, 2.4 g Sat); 71 mg Cholesterol; 12 g Carbohydrate; trace Fibre; 29 g Protein; 626 mg Sodium

balsamic raspberry chicken

Fast, low-fat and delicious—how can you go wrong? Serve with rice and salad.

Boneless, skinless chicken breast halves, cut into 1/2 inch (12 mm) strips	1 lb.	454 g
Dried sage	1/2 tsp.	2 mL
Dried thyme	1/2 tsp	2 mL
Salt	1/4 tsp.	1 mL
Pepper	1/4 tsp.	1 mL
Cooking oil	1 tsp.	5 mL
Balsamic vinegar	1/4 cup	60 mL
Raspberry jam	1/4 cup	60 mL
Orange juice	2 tbsp.	30 mL

Fresh raspberries, for garnish

Put chicken into medium bowl. Sprinkle with next 4 ingredients. Toss until coated.

Heat cooking oil in large frying pan on medium-high. Add chicken. Cook for 3 to 5 minutes, stirring often, until no longer pink. Transfer to plate. Cover to keep warm. Reduce heat to medium.

Add vinegar to same frying pan. Heat and stir for about 2 minutes, scraping any brown bits from bottom of pan, until vinegar is reduced by half. Add jam and orange juice. Heat and stir until jam is melted and sauce is thickened. Add chicken. Heat and stir for 1 to 2 minutes until heated through.

Garnish with raspberries. Makes about 2 cups (500 mL). Serves 4.

1 serving: 202 Calories; 3.0 g Total Fat (1.1 g Mono, 0.8 g Poly, 0.6 g Sat); 66 mg Cholesterol; 16 g Carbohydrate; trace Fibre; 26 g Protein; 214 mg Sodium

lemon ginger chicken

Did you know that room-temperature lemons yield more juice than refrigerated lemons? And, if you microwave the lemon for just a few seconds, you'll get more juice.

Boneless, skinless chicken breast halves	4	4
All-purpose flour	1/4 cup	60 mL
Salt	1/4 tsp.	1 mL
Pepper	1/4 tsp.	1 mL
Olive (or cooking) oil	2 tsp.	10 mL
Prepared chicken broth	1/2 cup	125 mL
Lemon juice	1/4 cup	60 mL
Brown sugar, packed	2 tbsp.	30 mL
Soy sauce	1 tbsp.	15 mL
Finely grated gingerroot	1 tsp.	5 mL
Grated lemon zest	1 tsp.	5 mL
Dry mustard	1/4 tsp.	1 mL
Prepared chicken broth	1/4 cup	60 mL
Cornstarch	1 1/2 tsp.	7 mL

Sprigs of fresh parsley, for garnish

Place chicken breasts between 2 sheets of plastic wrap. Pound with mallet or rolling pin to 1/4 inch (6 mm) thickness. Combine next 3 ingredients on large plate. Press both sides of chicken into flour mixture until coated.

Heat olive oil in large frying pan on medium-high. Add chicken. Cook for 2 to 4 minutes per side until no longer pink inside. Transfer to plate. Cover to keep warm. Reduce heat to medium.

Add next 7 ingredients to same frying pan. Heat and stir, scraping any brown bits from bottom of pan, until boiling.

Stir second amount of broth into cornstarch in small cup. Add to lemon juice mixture. Heat and stir until boiling and thickened. Reduce heat to medium-low. Add chicken. Turn to coat both sides. Cook for 1 to 2 minutes until heated through.

Garnish with parsley sprigs. Serves 4.

1 serving: 232 Calories; 4.8 g Total Fat (2.3 g Mono, 0.8 g Poly, 1.0 g Sat); 82 mg Cholesterol; 12 g Carbohydrate; trace Fibre; 33 g Protein; 632 mg Sodium

margo's rosemary chicken

If you want a thicker sauce, mix 1 1/2 tbsp. (25 mL) cornstarch in twice as much cold water and add it to the sauce, stirring constantly, until it boils. You can prepare it ahead of time and chill until ready to bake the chicken.

Cooking oil	2 tsp.	10 mL
Boneless, skinless chicken breast halves	10	10
Dry (or alcohol-free) white wine	1 cup	250 mL
Water	1 cup	250 mL
Red wine vinegar	1/3 cup	75 mL
Ketchup	1/4 cup	60 mL
Brown sugar, packed	2 tbsp.	30 mL
Grated onion	2 tbsp.	30 mL
Cornstarch	1 tbsp.	15 mL
Chicken bouillon powder	1 tsp.	5 mL
Dried dillweed	1 tsp.	5 mL
Dried rosemary	1 tsp.	5 mL
Dried oregano	1 tsp.	5 mL
Garlic clove, minced (or 1/4 tsp., 1 mL, powder)	1	1
Salt	1 tsp.	5 mL
Soy sauce	1 tsp.	5 mL
Worcestershire sauce	1 tsp.	5 mL
Paprika	1/2 tsp.	2 mL

Heat cooking oil in large frying pan on medium. Add chicken. Cook for about 4 minutes per side until browned. Transfer to ungreased 2 1/2 quart (2.5 L) casserole.

Combine remaining 16 ingredients in medium saucepan. Heat and stir on medium-high until boiling and slightly thickened. Pour over chicken. Bake, covered, in 350°F (175°C) oven for about 1 hour until chicken is no longer pink inside. Serves 10.

1 serving: 186 Calories; 2.5 g Total Fat (0.9 g Mono, 0.7 g Poly, 0.5 Sat); 68 mg Cholesterol; 6 g Carbohydrate; trace Fibre; 28 g Protein; 543 mg Sodium

kung pao chicken

If you like more heat, add extra sambal oelek. It's a multi-purpose condiment popular in Indonesia, Malaysia and Southern India. A blend of chilies, brown sugar and salt, sambal oelek is found in the Asian section of grocery stores.

Water	2 tbsp.	30 mL
Cornstarch	1 tbsp.	15 mL
Hoisin sauce	1 tbsp.	15 mL
Soy sauce	1 tbsp.	15 mL
Chili paste (sambal oelek)	1/2 tsp.	2 mL
Soy sauce	1 tbsp.	15 mL
Cornstarch	1 tbsp.	15 mL
Egg white (large), fork-beaten	1	1
Boneless, skinless chicken breast halves and thighs, diced	1 lb.	454 g
Sesame oil (for flavour)	1 tsp.	5 mL
Garlic clove, minced	1	1
Cooking oil	1 tbsp.	15 mL
Small carrots, thinly sliced	2	2
Garlic clove, minced	1	1
Finely grated gingerroot	1/2 tsp.	2 mL
Diced green pepper	1/2 cup	125 mL
Diced red pepper	1/2 cup	125 mL
Green onions, cut into 1 inch (2.5 cm) pieces	3	3
Fresh small red chili peppers (see Tip, page 64), optional	1 – 5	1 – 5
Cooking oil	1 tbsp.	15 mL
Chopped salted peanuts, for garnish		

Combine first 5 ingredients in small cup. Set aside.

Stir second amount of soy sauce into second amount of cornstarch in medium bowl.

Add next 4 ingredients. Stir well. Set aside.

Heat wok or large frying pan on medium-high until very hot. Add first amount of cooking oil. Add next 3 ingredients. Stir-fry for about 1 minute until carrots are tender-crisp.

Add next 4 ingredients. Stir-fry for 1 to 2 minutes until green and red pepper are tender-crisp. Transfer to separate medium bowl. Cover to keep warm.

Add second amount of cooking oil to hot wok. Add chicken mixture. Stir-fry for about 3 minutes until chicken is no longer pink. Stir hoisin sauce mixture. Add to chicken mixture. Heat and stir until boiling and thickened. Add pepper mixture. Heat and stir until peppers are heated through.

Garnish with peanuts. Makes about 4 cups (1 L). Serves 4.

1 serving: 249 Calories; 10.1 g Total Fat (4.9 g Mono, 3.0 g Poly, 1.2 g Sat); 66 mg Cholesterol; 11 g Carbohydrate; 1 g Fibre; 28 g Protein; 811 mg Sodium

fiery grilled chicken

*Making double this Aztec-inspired marinating paste takes you no more time, so
freeze an extra recipe of fresh chicken breasts right in the paste for a busy day.
Set it to thaw in the fridge in the morning and it will be ready when you get home.*

Lime juice	2 tbsp.	30 mL
Chopped fresh (or pickled) jalapeño pepper, (see Tip, page 64)	1 1/2 tbsp.	25 mL
Cocoa, sifted if lumpy	1 1/2 tbsp.	25 mL
Cooking oil	1 tbsp.	15 mL
Ground cumin	2 tsp.	10 mL
Dried crushed chilies	1 tsp.	5 mL
Granulated sugar	1 tsp.	5 mL
Ground cinnamon	3/4 tsp.	4 mL
Salt	3/4 tsp.	4 mL
Boneless, skinless chicken breast halves	6	6

Process first 9 ingredients in blender until smooth. Pour into large resealable
freezer bag.

Add chicken. Seal bag. Turn until coated. Let stand in refrigerator for at least
6 hours or overnight, turning occasionally. Preheat gas barbecue to medium.
Cook chicken on greased grill for about 8 to 10 minutes per side until no longer
pink inside. Serves 6.

1 serving: 158 Calories; 4.6 g Total Fat (1.9 g Mono, 1.1 g Poly, 0.8 g Sat); 66 mg Cholesterol;
3 g Carbohydrate; 1 g Fibre; 26 g Protein; 303 mg Sodium

italian colours

Here's a pretty presentation, with all the colours of the Italian flag! As an alternative, you can add the fresh basil just before serving.

All-purpose flour	1/3 cup	75 mL
Seasoned (or garlic) salt	1 tsp.	5 mL
Pepper, generous sprinkle		
Large egg	1	1
Olive (or cooking) oil	2 tbsp.	30 mL
Milk	1 tbsp.	15 mL
Fine dry bread crumbs	2/3 cup	150 mL
Chopped fresh parsley (or 1 tbsp., 15 mL, flakes)	1/4 cup	60 mL
Grated Parmesan cheese	3 tbsp.	50 mL
Boneless, skinless chicken breast halves	6	6
Provolone (or mozzarella) cheese slices	6	6
Tomato slices	6	6
Finely chopped fresh basil (or 1 1/2 tsp., 7 mL, dried)	2 tbsp.	30 mL

Combine first 3 ingredients in shallow dish.

Beat next 3 ingredients with a fork in small shallow bowl.

Combine next 3 ingredients in separate shallow dish.

Press both sides of chicken into flour mixture until coated. Dip into egg mixture. Press both sides into crumb mixture until coated. Arrange on greased baking sheet. Bake in 375°F (190°C) oven for about 25 minutes until no longer pink inside.

Layer remaining 3 ingredients, in order given, over chicken. Bake for about 5 minutes until cheese is melted. Serves 6.

1 serving: 343 Calories; 14.2 g Total Fat (6.1 g Mono, 1.4 g Poly, 5.4 g Sat); 117 mg Cholesterol; 17 g Carbohydrate; 1 g Fibre; 35 g Protein; 546 mg Sodium

mustard chicken pasta

A lively citrus tang flavours the rich, creamy sauce. If you're out of white wine, use apple juice instead.

Cooking oil	1 tbsp.	15 mL
Boneless, skinless chicken breast halves	4	4
Cooking oil	1 tbsp.	15 mL
Finely chopped onion	1 cup	250 mL
Garlic cloves, minced (or 1/2 tsp., 2 mL, powder)	2	2
Dry (or alcohol-free) white wine	1/2 cup	125 mL
Whipping cream	1 2/3 cups	400 mL
Dijon mustard (with whole seeds)	2 tbsp.	30 mL
Liquid honey	2 tbsp.	30 mL
Salt	1/4 tsp.	1 mL
Pepper	1/4 tsp.	1 mL
Frozen peas	2/3 cup	150 mL
Grated lemon zest	1 tsp.	5 mL
Chopped fresh parsley (or 2 1/4 tsp.,11 mL, flakes), optional	3 tbsp.	50 mL
Water	10 cups	2.5 L
Salt	1 1/2 tsp.	7 mL
Spinach fettuccine (or pasta of your choice)	8 oz.	225 g
Chopped fresh parsley, for garnish		

Heat first amount of cooking oil in large frying pan on medium. Add chicken. Cook for 3 to 4 minutes per side until browned. Chop coarsely. Set aside.

Heat second amount of cooking oil in same frying pan. Add onion and garlic. Cook for about 10 minutes, stirring often, until onion is softened.

Add wine. Bring to a boil. Boil, uncovered, for about 3 minutes until wine is reduced by half. Add next 5 ingredients. Stir. Reduce heat to medium. Boil gently for about 10 minutes, stirring occasionally, until thickened.

Add peas and chicken. Heat and stir for 5 to 6 minutes until chicken is no longer pink. Remove from heat.

Add lemon zest and parsley. Stir. Cover to keep warm.

Combine water and salt in Dutch oven. Bring to a boil. Add fettuccine. Boil, uncovered, for about 10 minutes, stirring occasionally, until tender but firm. Drain. Return to same pot. Add chicken mixture. Stir.

Garnish with parsley. Makes about 6 cups (1.5 L). Serves 6.

1 serving: 562 Calories; 29.7 g Total Fat (9.8 g Mono, 2.9 g Poly, 15 g Sat); 135 mg Cholesterol; 42 g Carbohydrate; 4 g Fibre; 29 g Protein; 229 mg Sodium

pepper chicken kabobs

Smoky grilled chicken and vegetables make an attractive and delicious main course for any barbecue party. If your garden is overflowing with zucchini you could thread a few slices onto your skewers.

Boneless, skinless chicken breast halves, cut into 24 equal pieces	1 lb.	454 g
Medium onion, cut into 24 equal pieces	1	1
Large yellow pepper, cut into 24 equal pieces	1	1
Large red pepper, cut into 24 equal pieces	1	1
Bamboo skewers (8 inches, 20 cm, each), soaked in water for 10 minutes	8	8

CITRUS PEPPER MARINADE		
Orange juice	1/2 cup	125 mL
Ranch dressing	1/4 cup	60 mL
Garlic cloves, minced (or 1/2 tsp., 2 mL, powder)	2	2
Grated lime zest	2 tsp.	10 mL
Ground cumin	1 tsp.	5 mL
Pepper	1 tsp.	5 mL

Thread first 4 ingredients alternately, in order given, onto skewers. Place in large shallow dish.

Citrus Pepper Marinade: Combine all 6 ingredients in small bowl. Makes about 1 cup (250 mL) marinade. Pour 2/3 cup (150 mL) over chicken kabobs. Refrigerate remaining marinade. Turn kabobs to coat. Let stand, covered, in refrigerator for 2 hours, turning occasionally. Preheat gas barbecue to medium-high. Cook on greased grill for about 6 minutes until browned on edges. Turn. Cook for about 6 minutes, brushing with reserved marinade, until chicken is no longer pink and vegetables are tender-crisp. Makes 8 kabobs.

1 kabob: 128 Calories; 5 g Total Fat (0.2 g Mono, 0.3 g Poly, 0.9 g Sat); 35 mg Cholesterol; 7 g Carbohydrate; 1 g Fibre; 14 g Protein; 105 mg Sodium

mediterranean chicken

Treat your guests to the flavours of the Mediterranean with tender, juicy chicken covered in a chunky rustic sauce of tomatoes, olives and oregano.

MEDITERRANEAN MARINADE

Chopped fresh oregano (or 1 tbsp., 15 mL, dried)	1/4 cup	60 mL
Dry (or alcohol-free) white wine	1/4 cup	60 mL
Olive oil	1/4 cup	60 mL
Lemon juice	2 tbsp.	30 mL
Garlic cloves, minced (or 1/2 tsp., 2 mL, powder)	2	2
Grated lemon zest	2 tsp.	10 mL
Liquid honey	2 tsp.	10 mL
Salt	1/4 tsp.	1 mL
Pepper	1/4 tsp.	1 mL

CHICKEN

Boneless skinless chicken breast halves	6	6
All-purpose flour	1/4 cup	60 mL
Olive oil	1 tbsp.	15 mL
Olive oil	1 tsp.	5 mL
Chopped onion	1 1/2 cups	375 mL
Can of diced tomatoes (with juice)	14 oz.	398 mL
Half-and-half cream	3 tbsp.	50 mL
Pitted whole black olives	3/4 cup	175 mL
Lemon slices	12	12
Chopped fresh oregano (or 1/2 tsp., 2 mL, dried)	2 tsp.	10 mL

Mediterranean Marinade: Combine all 9 ingredients in small bowl. Makes about 3/4 cup (175 mL) marinade.

Chicken: Put chicken into large resealable freezer bag. Add marinade. Seal bag. Turn to coat. Let stand in refrigerator for 1 to 2 hours, turning occasionally. Remove chicken. Reserve marinade. Pat chicken dry with paper towels.

Measure flour onto medium plate. Press both sides of chicken into flour until coated. Heat second amount of olive oil in large frying pan on medium-high. Add chicken. Cook chicken for 2 to 4 minutes per side until browned. Arrange chicken in single layer in ungreased 2 quart (2 L) casserole. Set aside. Reduce heat to medium.

Add third amount of olive oil to same frying pan. Add onion. Cook for 5 to 10 minutes, stirring often, until onion is softened.

Add tomatoes and reserved marinade. Bring to a boil. Reduce heat to medium-low. Simmer, uncovered, for 5 minutes to blend flavours.

Add cream and olives. Stir. Pour over chicken. Bake, covered, in 350°F (175°C) oven for about 30 minutes until bubbling and chicken is no longer pink inside.

Arrange lemon slices over chicken. Sprinkle with oregano. Serves 6.

1 serving: 358 Calories; 20 g Total Fat (9.6 g Mono, 1.5 g Poly, 2.7 g Sat); 69 mg Cholesterol; 16 g Carbohydrate; 1 g Fibre; 28 g Protein; 571 mg Sodium

rice crust chicken pie

Rice freezes beautifully, so you can cook extra to have on hand for this dish.

RICE CRUST		
Large egg, fork-beaten	1	1
Cooked long grain brown rice	3 cups	750 mL
Pepper	1/2 tsp.	2 mL
Grated mozzarella cheese	1 cup	250 mL

FILLING		
Cooking oil	1 tbsp.	15 mL
Boneless, skinless chicken breast halves, chopped	1/2 lb.	225 g
Sliced fresh white mushrooms	3 cups	750 mL
Chopped onion	1 cup	250 mL
Chopped red pepper	1 cup	250 mL
Garlic cloves, minced	2	2
All-purpose flour	2 tbsp.	30 mL
Dried basil	1/2 tsp.	2 mL
Dried oregano	1/4 tsp.	1 mL
Dried rosemary, crushed	1/4 tsp.	1 mL
Dry (or alcohol-free) white wine	1/2 cup	125 mL
Prepared chicken broth	1/2 cup	125 mL
Salt	1/8 tsp.	0.5 mL
Pepper	1/8 tsp.	0.5 mL
Grated Parmesan cheese	1/2 cup	125 mL

TOPPING		
Fine dry whole wheat bread crumbs	1/3 cup	75 mL
Butter (or hard margarine), melted	1 tbsp.	15 mL
Parsley flakes	1 tsp.	5 mL
Sprigs of fresh parsley, for garnish		

Rice crust: Combine first 3 ingredients in large bowl. Press firmly into bottom and 3/4 up side of greased 9 inch (22 cm) pie plate. Sprinkle cheese evenly over bottom. Bake in 350°F (175°C) for about 20 minutes until cheese is melted.

Filling: Heat cooking oil in large frying pan on medium-high. Add chicken. Cook for 3 to 5 minutes, stirring occasionally, until starting to brown. Remove to small bowl. Reduce heat to medium.

Add mushrooms and onion to same frying pan. Stir. Cook for about 5 minutes, stirring often, until onion starts to soften. Add red pepper and garlic. Stir. Cook for 2 minutes.

Sprinkle next 4 ingredients over mushroom mixture. Heat and stir for 1 minute. Add chicken. Stir. Add next 4 ingredients. Heat and stir for about 5 minutes until boiling and thickened.

Add cheese. Stir. Spread evenly in crust.

Topping: Combine all 3 ingredients in small cup. Sprinkle over filling. Bake, uncovered, in 350°F (175°C) oven for about 35 minutes until golden. Let stand for 5 minutes.

Garnish with parsley sprigs. Cuts into 6 wedges.

1 wedge: 363 Calories; 13.8 g Total Fat (4.8 g Mono, 1.7 g Poly, 13.8 g Sat); 80 mg Cholesterol; 34 g Carbohydrate; 3 g Fibre; 22 g Protein; 419 mg Sodium

chicken picadillo

A Spanish favourite, picadillo (pronounced pee-kah-DEE-yoh) makes great use of common kitchen spices. Slicing the chicken breast at a 45° angle will allow it to cook quickly, but still remain tender.

Boneless, skinless chicken breast halves, cut into 3/4 inch (2 cm) strips	1 lb.	454 g	
Salt	1/4 tsp.	1 mL	
Pepper	1/8 tsp.	0.5 mL	
Ground cumin	1 tsp.	5 mL	
Dried basil	1/2 tsp.	2 mL	
Dried oregano	1/2 tsp.	2 mL	
Garlic powder	1/4 tsp.	1 mL	
Ground cinnamon	1/4 tsp.	1 mL	
Salt	1/4 tsp.	1 mL	
Olive (or cooking) oil	2 tbsp.	30 mL	
Chopped onion	1/4 cup	60 mL	
Tomato paste (see Tip, page 64)	1 tbsp.	15 mL	
Dry (or alcohol-free) red wine	1/4 cup	60 mL	
Can of diced tomatoes (with juice)	14 oz.	398 mL	
Sliced green olives	1/2 cup	125 mL	
Brown sugar, packed	1 tbsp.	15 mL	
Fresh oregano, for garnish			

Sprinkle chicken with salt and pepper.

Combine next 6 ingredients in small cup. Set aside.

Heat olive oil in large frying pan on medium-high. Cook chicken in 2 batches, for about 2 minutes per batch, stirring occasionally, until starting to brown. Transfer to plate. Cover to keep warm.

Add onion to same frying pan. Cook for about 5 minutes, stirring often, until softened.

Add tomato paste and spice mixture. Heat and stir for about 1 minute until fragrant. Add wine. Heat and stir for about 1 minute, scraping any brown bits from bottom of pan, until mixture resembles paste.

Add next 3 ingredients and chicken. Stir. Reduce heat to medium-low. Cook, covered, for about 5 minutes until heated through and chicken is no longer pink.

Garnish with oregano. Makes about 4 cups (1 L). Serves 4.

1 Serving: 496 Calories; 18.8 g Total Fat (10.5 g Mono, 2.9 g Poly, 3.7 g Sat); 169 mg Cholesterol; 11 g Carbohydrate; 2 g Fibre; 64 g Protein; 1274 mg Sodium

brandied chicken

The evaporated skim milk gives this entree a creamy richness without the calories.

Cooking oil	2 tsp.	10 mL
Boneless, skinless chicken breast halves	6	6
Salt, sprinkle		
Pepper, sprinkle		
Sliced fresh white mushrooms	2 cups	500 mL
Skim evaporated milk	1/2 cup	125 mL
Brandy	1 tsp.	5 mL

Heat cooking oil in large frying pan on medium. Add chicken. Cook for about 10 to 15 minutes per side until chicken is no longer pink inside. Sprinkle with salt and pepper. Remove chicken to platter. Cover to keep warm.

Add mushrooms to same frying pan. Cook for about 5 to 10 minutes until liquid is evaporated, stirring occasionally.

Add evaporated milk and brandy. Heat and stir, scraping any brown bits from bottom of pan, until almost boiling. Spoon over chicken. Serves 6.

1 serving: 169 Calories; 3.2 g Total Fat (1.3 g Mono, 0.8 g Poly, 0.5 g Sat); 69 mg Cholesterol; 4 g Carbohydrate; trace Fibre; 29 g Protein; 104 mg Sodium

stuffed chicken rolls

A slow cooker makes it easy to look forward to this great dish after a long workday. The well-seasoned sauce is wonderful over mashed potatoes or rice.

Boneless, skinless chicken breast halves	6	6
Thin deli ham slices, cut to fit chicken	6	6
Hot water	1/2 cup	125 mL
Dry (or alcohol-free) white wine	1/2 cup	125 mL
Chicken bouillon powder	2 tsp.	10 mL
Dried marjoram	1/2 tsp.	2 mL
Salt	1/2 tsp.	2 mL
Pepper	1/4 tsp.	1 mL
Liquid gravy browner (optional)	1 tsp.	5 mL
Grated Swiss cheese	1 cup	250 mL
Water	2 1/2 tbsp.	37 mL
Cornstarch	1 tbsp.	15 mL

Place 1 chicken breast between 2 sheets of plastic wrap. Pound with mallet or rolling pin to 1/2 inch (5 cm) thickness. Place 1 ham slice on chicken breast. Roll up tightly, jelly roll-style. Secure with wooden picks. Repeat with remaining chicken and ham. Arrange in 3 1/2 to 4 quart (3.5 to 4 L) slow cooker.

Combine next 7 ingredients in small bowl. Pour over chicken rolls. Cook, covered, on Low for 8 to 9 hours or on High for 4 to 4 1/2 hours. Transfer chicken rolls to serving dish with slotted spoon or tongs.

Sprinkle cheese over chicken rolls. Cover to keep warm.

Stir water into cornstarch in small cup. Add to slow cooker. Stir. Cook, covered, on High for about 15 minutes, stirring occasionally, until boiling and slightly thickened. Serve with chicken rolls. Serves 6.

1 serving: 414 Calories; 10.0 g Total Fat (1.1 g Mono, 1.0 g Poly, 4.5 g Sat); 182 mg Cholesterol; 3 g Carbohydrate; trace Fibre; 69 g Protein; 1057 mg Sodium

chicken cordon bleu

The classic dish is usually pan-fried, but we've adapted it so you can throw it into the oven and grab a few minutes for yourself. If you'd like to follow the more traditional method, just continue cooking the chicken rolls in the frying pan until they're no longer pink inside.

Boneless, skinless chicken breast halves	6	6
Salt, sprinkle		
Deli cooked ham slices	6	6
Swiss cheese, cut into 6 sticks	6 oz.	170 g
All-purpose flour	1/4 cup	60 mL
Hard margarine (not butter)	2 tbsp.	30 mL
Chicken bouillon cubes (1/5 oz., 6 g, each)	3	3
Boiling water	1/2 cup	125 mL
Can of sliced mushrooms, drained	10 oz.	284 mL
Dry (or alcohol-free) white wine	1/3 cup	75 mL
All-purpose flour	2 tbsp.	30 mL
Water	1/2 cup	125 mL
Slivered almonds, toasted (see Tip, page 64)	1/2 cup	125 mL

Place 1 chicken breast between 2 sheets of plastic wrap. Pound with mallet or rolling pin to 1/4 inch (6 mm) thickness. Sprinkle with salt. Lay 1 ham slice on top of chicken piece. Lay cheese stick over ham. Roll up tightly, jelly roll-style. Secure with wooden picks. Repeat with remaining chicken, ham and cheese. Press rolls into first amount of flour until coated. Let stand, covered, for 20 minutes.

Melt margarine in medium frying pan on medium. Add rolls. Cook for about 10 minutes, turning several times, until browned. Arrange in single layer in ungreased 2 quart (2 L) casserole.

Dissolve bouillon cubes in boiling water in same frying pan. Add mushrooms and wine. Pour over rolls. Bake, covered, in 350°F (175°C) oven for 1 to 1 1/2 hours until chicken is no longer pink inside. Remove rolls to platter. Cover to keep warm.

Transfer liquid to medium saucepan. Bring to a boil. Reduce heat to medium. Stir second amount of flour into water in small cup until smooth. Add to liquid. Heat and stir until boiling and thickened. Pour over chicken. Scatter almonds over top. Serves 6.

1 serving: 425 Calories; 23.9 g Total Fat (11.1 g Mono, 3 g Poly, 8.2 g Sat); 95 mg Cholesterol; 13 g Carbohydrate; 2 g Fibre; 37 g Protein; 1245 mg Sodium

chicken breast florentine

Nutmeg and spinach make a beautiful pairing in this dish. Grating a fresh nutmeg will allow you to revel in the complex aromas of this exotic spice.

Plain yogurt	1/2 cup	125 mL
Sour cream	1/2 cup	125 mL
Dry mustard	1 1/2 tsp.	7 mL
Dried dillweed	1/2 tsp.	2 mL
Fine dry bread crumbs	1 1/2 cups	375 mL
Boneless, skinless chicken breast halves	8	8

FLORENTINE SAUCE

Butter (or hard margarine)	1/4 cup	60 mL
All-purpose flour	1/4 cup	60 mL
Dried dillweed	2 tsp.	10 mL
Chicken bouillon powder	1 tsp.	5 mL
Ground nutmeg	1/4 tsp.	1 mL
Onion powder	1/4 tsp.	1 mL
Salt	1 tsp.	5 mL
Pepper	1/4 tsp.	1 mL
Milk	3 cups	750 mL
Box of frozen chopped spinach, thawed and squeezed dry	10 oz.	300 g

Grated havarti or Muenster cheese	1 cup	250 mL

Mix first 4 ingredients in small bowl. Put bread crumbs into small shallow dish. Dip chicken into sour cream mixture. Press both sides into bread crumbs until coated. Arrange in single layer on greased baking sheet. Bake in 375°F (190°C) oven for 35 to 45 minutes, turning at halftime, until no longer pink inside.

Florentine Sauce: Melt butter in medium saucepan on medium. Sprinkle with next 7 ingredients. Heat and stir for 1 minute.

Slowly add milk, stirring constantly. Add spinach. Heat and stir until boiling and thickened. Reduce heat to medium-low. Simmer, uncovered, for 3 minutes, stirring often.

Stir in cheese until melted. Place chicken on platter or dinner plates. Spoon sauce over top. Serves 8.

1 serving: 419 Calories; 17.6 g Total Fat (5.1 g Mono, 1.1 g Poly, 9.8 g Sat); 109 mg Cholesterol; 26 g Carbohydrate; 2 g Fibre; 38 g Protein; 921 mg Sodium

elegant chicken phyllo

Multiply this recipe by the number of servings you'll need. If you prepare this in the morning, brush the phyllo with melted butter and cover with plastic wrap before refrigerating.

Phyllo pastry sheets, thawed according to package directions	2	2
Hard margarine (or butter), melted	1 tbsp.	15 mL
Light spreadable cream cheese, mashed with fork	1 tbsp.	15 mL
Chopped pimiento	1 1/2 tsp.	7 mL
Boneless, skinless chicken breast half, pounded flat and cut into thin strips	1	1
Salt, sprinkle		
Pepper, sprinkle		
Medium fresh white mushroom, sliced	1	1

Lay 1 sheet of pastry on working surface. Brush sheet with melted margarine. Fold in half crosswise. Repeat with second pastry sheet. Place second sheet crosswise over first sheet.

Spread cream cheese in 4 inch (10 cm) diameter circle in centre of pastry. Layer next 5 ingredients in order given, over top. Gather ends of pastry sheets and press together at top of filling to enclose, allowing corners to flare outward. Place on greased baking sheet. Bake in 350°F (175°C) oven for about 30 minutes until pastry is browned and crisp. Serve immediately. Serves 1.

1 serving: 409 Calories; 15.8 g Total Fat (8.6 g Mono, 1.9 g Poly, 4.2 g Sat); 76 mg Cholesterol; 32 g Carbohydrate; 1 g Fibre; 33 g Protein; 619 mg Sodium

spinach-stuffed chicken

A true, special-occasion dish. You can stuff and refrigerate the chicken breast four hours ahead. Chill the butter up to five days, or freeze up to three months.

CITRUS HERB BUTTER

Butter (or hard margarine), softened	1/4 cup	60 mL
Chopped fresh chives	1 1/2 tsp.	7 mL
Chopped fresh parsley	1 1/2 tsp.	7 mL
Grated lime zest	1 tsp.	5 mL
Grated orange zest	1 tsp.	5 mL
Lime juice	1/2 tsp.	2 mL

SPINACH-STUFFED CHICKEN

Cooking oil	1 tsp.	5 mL
Finely chopped onion	1/2 cup	125 mL
Garlic clove, minced (or 1/4 tsp., 1 mL, powder)	1	1
Ground cumin	1/2 tsp.	2 mL
Ground nutmeg, just a pinch		
Box of frozen chopped spinach, thawed and squeezed dry	10 oz.	300 g
Crumbled feta cheese	1/2 cup	125 mL
Boneless, skinless chicken breast halves	6	6
Cooking oil	2 tsp.	10 mL

Citrus Herb Butter: Beat butter in small bowl until smooth. Add remaining 5 ingredients. Beat well. Chill, covered, for about 40 minutes until butter is firm but not hard. Roll into 3 inch (7.5 cm) long log. Wrap with plastic wrap. Chill until ready to serve. Cuts into six 1/2 inch (12 mm) slices.

Spinach-Stuffed Chicken: Heat first amount of cooking oil in large frying pan on medium. Add onion. Cook for about 5 minutes, stirring often, until softened.

Add next 3 ingredients. Heat and stir for about 1 minute until fragrant. Add spinach. Cook for about 2 minutes, stirring occasionally, until liquid is evaporated. Remove from heat. Stir in cheese until melted. Transfer to small bowl. Chill, covered, for about 1 hour until cold.

Cut deep pocket in thickest part of chicken breasts almost, but not quite through, to other side. Spoon spinach mixture into pockets.

Heat second amount of cooking oil in separate large frying pan on medium-high. Add chicken. Cook for 2 to 3 minutes per side until browned. Transfer to greased baking sheet with sides. Bake in 375°F (190°C) oven for about 20 minutes until chicken is no longer pink inside and meat thermometer inserted into centre of stuffing reads 165°F (74°C). Remove from oven. Let stand, covered, for 5 minutes. Top with Citrus Herb Butter slices. Serves 6.

1 serving: 302 Calories; 15.9 g Total Fat (4.9 g Mono, 1.7 g Poly, 12.9 g Sat); 116 mg Cholesterol; 4 g Carbohydrate; 2 g Fibre; 35 g Protein; 267 mg Sodium

recipe index

topical tips

Bacterial prevention: It is important to clean the cutting board and any utensils used to cut raw chicken, fish or meat in hot, soapy water immediately after use. This will prevent bacteria from spreading to other food.

Handling hot peppers: Hot peppers contain capsaicin in the seeds and ribs. Removing the seeds and ribs will reduce the heat. Wear rubber gloves when handling hot peppers and avoid touching your eyes. Wash your hands well afterwards.

Toasting nuts, seeds or coconut: Cooking times will vary for each type of nut, so never toast them together. For small amounts, place ingredient in an ungreased shallow frying pan. Heat on medium for three to five minutes, stirring often, until golden. For larger amounts, spread ingredient evenly in an ungreased shallow pan. Bake in a 350ºF (175ºC) oven for five to 10 minutes, stirring or shaking often, until golden.

Tomato paste leftovers: If a recipe calls for less than an entire can of tomato paste, freeze the unopened can for 30 minutes. Open both ends and push the contents through one end. Slice off only what you need. Freeze the remaining paste in a resealable freezer bag or plastic wrap for future use.

Zest first; juice second: When a recipe calls for grated zest and juice, it's easier to grate the lemon or lime first, then juice it. Be careful not to grate down to the pith (white part of the peel), which is bitter and best avoided.

Nutrition Information Guidelines

Each recipe is analyzed using the Canadian Nutrient File from Health Canada, which is based on the United States Department of Agriculture (USDA) Nutrient Database.

- If more than one ingredient is listed (such as "butter or hard margarine"), or if a range is given (1 – 2 tsp., 5 – 10 mL), only the first ingredient or first amount is analyzed.

- For meat, poultry and fish, the serving size per person is based on the recommended 4 oz. (113 g) uncooked weight (without bone), which is 2 – 3 oz. (57 – 85 g) cooked weight (without bone) — approximately the size of a deck of playing cards.

- Milk used is 1% M.F. (milk fat), unless otherwise stated.

- Cooking oil used is canola oil, unless otherwise stated.

- Ingredients indicating "sprinkle," "optional," or "for garnish" are not included in the nutrition information.

- The fat in recipes and combination foods can vary greatly depending on the sources and types of fats used in each specific ingredient. For these reasons, the count of saturated, monounsaturated and polyunsaturated fats may not add up to the total fat content.